Southern Sky.
$39.09

World in Focus
Indonesia

SALLY MORGAN

WAYLAND

First published in 2007 by Wayland, an imprint of Hachette Children's Books

Hachette Children's Books, 338 Euston Road, London NW1 3BH

Wayland Australia, Hachette Children's Books, Level 17/207 Kent Street, Sydney, NSW 2000

Commissioning editor: Nicola Edwards
Editor: Patience Coster
Inside design: Chris Halls, www.mindseyedesign.co.uk
Cover design: Wayland
Series concept and project management by EASI-Educational Resourcing
(info@easi-er.co.uk)

Statistical research: Anna Bowden
Maps and graphs: Martin Darlison, Encompass Graphics

British Library Cataloguing in Publication Data
Morgan, Sally
    Indonesia - (World in focus)
    1. Indonesia - Juvenile literature
    I. Title
    959.8'04

ISBN-13: 9780750247474

Printed and bound in China

Cover top: The fertile slopes near the village of Ubud are worked by hand as it is difficult to get machinery on to the terraces.
Cover bottom and title page: In Denpasar, Bali, dancers with elaborate headdresses take part in the Melasti ceremony, in which the victory of good over evil is celebrated.

The author and publisher would like to thank the following for allowing their pictures to be reproduced in this publication: Alamy 43 (Vince Bevan); Corbis 4 (Nik Wheeler), 5 (Anders Ryman), 6 (Beawiharta/Reuters), 8 (WEDA/epa), 9 (Stapleton Collection), 10, 11 (Bettmann), 12 (Crack Palinggi/Reuters), 13 (Reuters), 16 (Stephen Frink), 17 (Owen Franken), 18 (Wolfgang Kaehler), 19 (Sergio Dorantes), 22 (Kevin Lamarque/Reuters), 23 (Bagus Indahono/epa), 24 (Beawiharta/Reuters), 25 (Jacqueline M. Koch), 27 (Justin Guariglia), 28 (Wolfgang Kaehler), 30 (Supri/Reuters), 31 (Tarmizy Harva/Reuters), 32 (Supri/Reuters), 33 (Crack Palinggi/Reuters), 34 (POOL/Reuters), 35 (Reuters), 36 (Reuters), 37 (Lirio Da Fonseca/Reuters), 38 (James Robert Fuller), 39 (Beawiharta/Reuters), 41 (Kaveh Kazemi), 42 (Tarmizy Harva/Reuters), 44 (Crack Palinggi/Reuters), 45 (Lindsay Hebberd), 46 and title page (Mast Irham/epa), 47 (Free Agents Limited), 48 (Barry Lewis), 49 (Supri/Reuters), 51 (Reuters), 52 (Stuart Westmorland), 53 (Stuart Westmorland), 54 (Wolfgang Kaehler), 56 (Mast Irham/epa), 57 (Robert Harding World Imagery), 59 (Tarmizy Harva/Reuters); Corbis Sygma 26 (Jufri Kemal); EASI-Images/Simon Scoones 14, 15; EASI-Images/Ed Parker 20, 29, 55; EASI-Images/Clive Sanders 21; EASI-Images/Jenny Matthews 40, 58; EASI-Images/Neal Cavalier-Smith 50.

The directional arrow portrayed on the map on page 7 provides only an approximation of north.

The data used to produce the graphics and data panels in this title were the latest available at the time of production.

CONTENTS

CHAPTER 1

Indonesia – An Overview

Indonesia is the largest archipelago in the world, formed from 17,508 islands. The Indonesian archipelago extends for more than 5,000 km (3,107 miles) between the Asian and Australian mainlands. Indonesia is the world's fourth most populous country after China, India and the USA. In 2006, there were over 245 million people living in a land area of 1,826,440 sq km (705,006 sq miles), which is almost three times the size of the US state of Texas. Strategically, Indonesia is one of the most important nations in South-east Asia, as it is positioned at the crossroads between the Asian and Australian continents and between the Indian and Pacific oceans. One of the most important sea routes in the world, a narrow stretch of water called the Straits of Malacca lies between Sumatra, the westernmost island of Indonesia, and Malaysia. More than 50,000 vessels pass through the straits each year, carrying up to a quarter of the world's sea trade, including oil for China and Japan.

A DIVERSE NATION

Millions of years ago, there was a land bridge between the Indonesian islands and Asia. Early man could therefore walk between one and the other. One million years ago, the sea level rose and cut Indonesia off from the mainland but this did not stop people reaching the islands. During the last few thousand years, immigrant

◀ The thousands of islands create a long and varied coastline. There are many sandy beaches, rugged cliffs and forests that run down to the sea.

peoples have travelled to Indonesia by boat from Malaysia, Thailand and Vietnam and from Melanesia in the east, bringing with them their cultures and languages.

Indonesia's national motto is 'Unity in Diversity'. This reflects the fact that the population is made up of more than 300 ethnic groups, each with its own language and culture. However, these diverse groups are drawn together by their common language, Bahasa Indonesia, which is spoken throughout the islands. Although this great diversity has enriched the culture, it has made governing Indonesia very difficult.

Between 1623 and 1942, Indonesia was controlled by the Dutch (see page 9). The Japanese invaded in 1942 and remained until

▲ In June 2000 on the island of Bali, members of a local Hindu temple carry out a purification rite on the beach. Women carry sacred objects on their heads as part of the temple's anniversary celebrations.

1945. The Dutch returned in 1945, and for the next four years there were hostilities between the Dutch and the Indonesians. Indonesia finally gained its independence in 1949. Governing Indonesia has not been straightforward. Successive governments have been beset by problems such as corruption, human rights abuses and poverty. Ethnic unrest

 Did you know?

The name Indonesia has its roots in two Greek words: 'Indos' meaning 'Indian' and 'Nesos' which means 'islands'.

◄ In the early morning on a busy street in the Indonesian capital, Jakarta, a young boy sleeps on the pavement while people go about their daily business. Despite government programmes to fight poverty, homelessness is still a problem in the major cities.

in the provinces of Aceh (at the northern tip of Sumatra), Papua and East Timor (islands in the far east) has meant that Indonesia's recent history is quite bloody.

The country has only just emerged from four decades of authoritarianism during which the military was powerful, free speech was restricted and human rights were not respected. Today there is a democratically elected

president and a government that is beginning to implement reforms. However, the challenges confronting Indonesia include corruption, widespread poverty, ethnic unrest, demands for more self-rule, and the fight against terrorism.

Did you know?

The red bar on the Indonesian flag symbolizes human blood and bravery, and the white bar represents the human spirit, peace and honesty. The colours and design are based on the flag used by the once powerful Hindu Majapahit Empire, which ruled Java (the main island of the Indonesian archipelago) during the thirteenth century. The Majapahit Empire flag had nine red and white stripes.

Physical geography

- ▭ Land area: 1,826,440 sq km/705,006 sq miles
- ▭ Water area: 93,000 sq km/35,898 sq miles
- ▭ Total area: 1,919,440 sq km/740,904 sq miles
- ▭ World rank (by area): 17
- ▭ Land boundaries: 2,830 km/1,759 miles
- ▭ Border countries: East Timor, Malaysia, Papua New Guinea
- ▭ Coastline: 54,716 km/34,000 miles
- ▭ Highest point: Puncak Jaya (5,030 m/16,503 ft)
- ▭ Lowest point: Indian Ocean (0 m/0 ft)

Source: CIA World Factbook

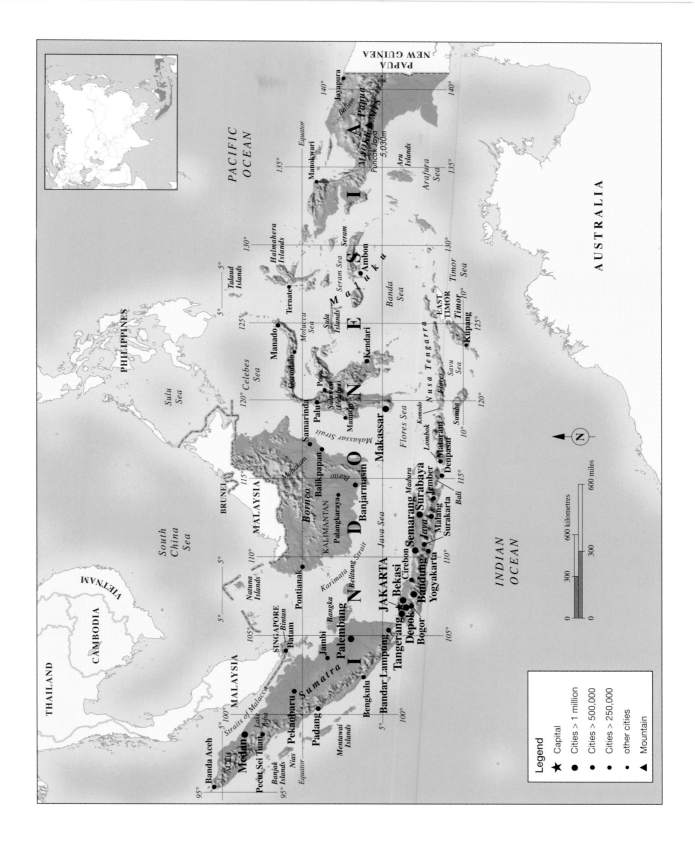

CHAPTER 2

History

The history of the Indonesian islands stretches back for 1.6 million years. Scientists have discovered fossils of a human ancestor – Java Man (*Homo erectus*) – who lived in east Java (a major Indonesian island) at that time. Several thousand years ago, people moved into the region from islands to the east. Ever since that time, migrants have arrived in Indonesia from India, the Middle East and Europe.

THE BUDDHIST AND HINDU KINGDOMS

Two thousand years ago, Indian traders and Buddhist and Hindu monks arrived in the islands. By the seventh and eighth centuries a number of regions in Sumatra and Java were ruled by local kings who had adopted the Hindu or Buddhist faiths. These kings introduced Indian culture and customs to Indonesia, including architecture, music and dance. Between the seventh and thirteenth centuries, Sumatra was the centre of an important Buddhist kingdom called Sri Vijaya. However, by the end of the thirteenth century the seat of power had shifted from Sumatra to Java, where the Hindu kingdom of Majapahit was powerful. For the next two hundred years, the Majapahit Empire ruled over much of Indonesia and present-day Malaysia.

THE ARRIVAL OF ISLAM

During the fourteenth and fifteenth centuries, Muslim Arab traders arrived from North Africa and the Middle East via Malacca, an important trading centre on mainland Malaysia. Gradually, the Majapahits retreated to Bali, a small island to the east of Java. By the sixteenth century, Java and Sumatra had become part of a Muslim empire with Islam as the main religion. The former Hindu kingdoms were divided into smaller Islamic states.

EUROPEAN TRADERS

As far as we know, the first European person to visit Indonesia was the Italian explorer, Marco Polo, who landed by ship in Sumatra in about 1292. Other European traders followed, searching for spices that were highly prized in

▶ The Borobodur temple dates back to the ninth century and is the largest Buddhist monument in South-east Asia. Buddhist monks gather here to celebrate Vesakh Day, the most important day in the Buddhist calendar.

◀ This illustration shows French explorers on a 'round-the-world' voyage at a boatyard near Kupang on the island of Timor in about 1820.

Europe. The Portuguese set up trading centres in the Maluku islands in north-east Indonesia in the early sixteenth century. The Dutch followed in 1596, and the English in 1600.

However, the Europeans were soon fighting one another over the valuable spice trade. By 1623 the Dutch had emerged as the most powerful group and they forced the Portuguese to retreat to East Timor and the English to other parts of South-east Asia.

DUTCH RULE

Over the next 170 years, the Dutch East India Company extended its control over the islands. The local people tried, unsuccessfully, to force the Dutch out. In 1740, Chinese traders and local Indonesians started a rebellion in Jakarta, but it was quashed by the Dutch who killed thousands of Chinese people. In 1799, the Dutch government seized control and the region became known as the Dutch East Indies. The island of Bali remained independent until 1906, when Dutch soldiers invaded and killed thousands of Balinese people.

THE NOVEMBER PROMISE

In 1918, the Dutch promised to grant self-government to the Indonesians. This was known as the 'November promise', but it was never fulfilled. As a compromise, the Dutch set up a body called the Volksraad, which was supposed to give more self-rule to the people, but it was powerless. By 1923, there was great unrest among the Indonesian people.

 Did you know?

In 2004, a new species of human called *Homo floresiensis* was discovered in a limestone cave on the Indonesian island of Flores. The 18,000-year-old skeleton was that of an adult just 1 m (3.28 ft) tall. It is thought that *Homo floresiensis* reached Flores using bamboo rafts and may have lived in remote areas until a few thousand years ago.

In the 1920s, the financial problems of the USA and Europe had spread to Indonesia and the people went on strike in protest over rising levels of unemployment and poverty. The Dutch colonial government responded by censoring newspapers and restricting the freedom of the people, preventing them from gathering in public places. In July 1927, the Parti Nasional Indonesia (Indonesian Nationalist Party), or PNI, was formed. It was a militant group that refused to co-operate with the Dutch colonial government. The Dutch responded by putting some of its leaders, including Achmed Sukarno and Muhammad Hatta, in jail.

An opportunity for change came during the Second World War. In 1942 the Japanese army invaded the Dutch East Indies and Sukarno and Hatta were released from jail. But it soon became clear that the Japanese were not prepared to give the Indonesians their independence, instead they wanted to rule the islands. The Indonesian people started to undermine Japanese control by attacking their supply lines and garrisons. Finally the Japanese allowed the Indonesians to carry out much of their country's administration.

INDEPENDENCE

The end of the Second World War in the Pacific came in August 1945, when the Japanese army surrendered to the Western allies. Immediately, Sukarno and Hatta declared Indonesia an independent republic. But their triumph was short-lived: within days, Dutch troops had landed to reclaim power. The Indonesians resisted and for the next four years there was heavy fighting between the two sides. Finally, in November 1949 the United Nations (UN) managed to get the opponents to agree to Indonesian independence. A new constitution was drawn up, Sukarno was elected president and Hatta became prime minister.

SUKARNO'S RULE

Sukarno had managed what had seemed impossible – the unification of a very diverse group of people under one government and one language, Bahasa Indonesia. But his government was inefficient and there was widespread corruption and administrative chaos. During the late 1950s, Sukarno expelled many of the Dutch colonists and claimed their property. The Dutch colonists controlled many of the businesses and owned much of the land,

► In 1944, during the Second World War, US forces landed along the northern coast of Dutch New Guinea. Here amphibious tanks have come ashore at Cape Sansapor.

▶ President Sukarno talking to an angry crowd in Jakarta on 17 October 1952. The demonstration had been organized by senior members of the military who wanted to give Sukarno a reason to dissolve parliament. He refused and in the months that followed replaced senior army officers with men more likely to do his bidding.

so their departure severely disrupted the economy. Unemployment rose and there was great economic hardship among the people. In 1958, a rebellion started in Sumatra when the people of this region demanded more independence. The unrest spread to Sulawesi and other islands. Sukarno used the army to put down the rebellion and his rule became stronger and more authoritarian. In 1960 he dissolved parliament and took control of the country. This marked the beginning of Sukarno's rule without a democratically elected government. At the same time, the Communist Party was growing in popularity; soon the two most powerful groups in Indonesia were the army and the Communist Party.

Focus on: East Timor

The province of East Timor gained independence from the Portuguese in 1975, but was immediately taken over by Indonesia, a move not recognized by the United Nations. In the following years, separatists of the mostly Roman Catholic province resisted Indonesian control. Indonesian troops moved in and there was loss of life on both sides. The USA and human rights organizations voiced criticism of Indonesia over the way it abused indigenous people in East Timor.

In 1999, Indonesia reluctantly agreed to allow a referendum so that the East Timorese people could choose between limited self-rule within Indonesia and independence – they chose independence. This result triggered months of violence, during which the Indonesian army and armed militias carried out a campaign of terror against the people, forcing thousands to flee their homes. Finally the United Nations sent in a peacekeeping force to take over until 2002, when the country finally became independent.

THE FALL OF SUKARNO

In September 1965, the Communist Party tried to weaken the power of the army by assassinating six high-ranking officers. There was violence in the streets as students demonstrated against the communists. In the months that followed, many alleged communists were killed, including thousands of Indonesian Chinese. Finally, in 1966, Sukarno gave General Soeharto supreme authority to bring the country to order.

THE SOEHARTO ERA

Once order had been resumed, Soeharto banned the Communist Party and appointed a new government with himself as chief executive. In 1967, Sukarno was voted out of power and Soeharto became president. He was re-elected in 1973, 1978, 1983, 1988, 1993, and again in 1998. However, in these elections Soeharto was the only candidate. Although he improved the economy of the country, he ruled with an 'iron fist'. Opposition parties were prevented from having a voice and government corruption grew worse. Soeharto's downfall came in 1997, when the Indonesian currency had to be devalued during the Asian Currency Crisis (see page 31). The unstable situation led to riots as inflation and unemployment soared, and there was a public outcry for Soeharto to resign. Although he was re-elected in 1998, Soeharto resigned almost immediatey and was replaced by Vice President B. J. Habibie.

In 1999, Abdurrahman Wahid became president. Wahid had campaigned on a pledge to fight corruption, but a few years later corruption scandals forced him to step down. In 2001, Megawati Sukarnoputri (Sukarno's daughter) was elected president. During her presidency, the government granted limited self-rule to the provinces of Aceh and Papua. It was hoped that this would end the fighting in these regions, but it did not. Peace talks in Aceh failed and the army moved in again in 2003.

▶ President Megawati Sukarnoputri came to power in 2001. She is shown here visiting the Jakarta Stock Exchange in April 2004, just days before she was defeated in the general election.

Corruption continued to undermine Megawati Sukarnoputri's government too, and she was defeated in an election in 2004. Her successor was Susilo Bambang Yudhoyono. His election was the first time that Indonesians had been able to elect a president directly. Previously the president had been elected indirectly, by the legislature.

Focus on: The troubled province of Aceh

Although the people of Aceh province in north Sumatra are Muslim, their culture is different from the rest of Indonesia. Since 1976, separatists of the Free Aceh Movement have fought a campaign for independence. During this time, the Indonesian government has been unwilling to give the province independence because it wants to retain possession of Aceh's rich natural resources. In 2003, government troops moved in to crush the rebels and the fighting between the two sides continued until 2005. On 26 December 2004, an earthquake off the coast of Sumatra created a tsunami (tidal wave) that devastated Aceh, killing about 130,000 people and making half a million people homeless. The tsunami was the trigger for more peace talks and, in August 2005, Acehnese rebels and the Indonesian government signed a peace agreement to end the violence. The rebels agreed to disarm and stop their campaign for independence in exchange for more self-rule. Aceh is not the only province to have called for more independence. There have also been uprisings in East Timor, Kalimantan (part of the island of Borneo) and Papua.

▶ In August 2002 Indonesian soldiers leave Aceh province after completing a three month long tour of duty. Since 1976, thousands of Indonesian soldiers have been sent to the region to fight the separatists and thousands have lost their lives on both sides.

CHAPTER 3

Landscape and Climate

Indonesia is a nation of many islands, of which about 6,000 are inhabited. The largest islands are Java, Sumatra and Sulawesi. Other major provinces include Kalimantan (which makes up 60 per cent of the island of Borneo), and Papua (part of the island of New Guinea). Papua was formerly a Dutch colony, but it was invaded by the Indonesian army in 1962 and has been under Indonesian control ever since. Many of the islands have mountainous interiors surrounded by coastal plains. The highest point in Indonesia is Mount Puncak Jaya in Papua, at 5,030 m (16,503 ft).

VOLCANIC ACTIVITY

Indonesia forms part of the 'Ring of Fire', a vast circle of volcanoes located around the edge of the Pacific Ocean. There are more than 400 volcanoes in Indonesia, of which 130 are active. Most of them lie in a chain stretching from northern Sumatra through the islands of Java, Bali, Lombok and Flores. About 70 of these volcanoes have erupted during the past 500 years. Mount Merapi, near Yogyakarta, is considered to be the most violent of the active volcanoes. It erupted last in June 2006.

Indonesia lies in an earthquake zone and many areas experience minor tremors every year. The destructive tsunami of December 2004 was the result of a huge underwater earthquake which caused violent movements in the ocean and created a huge tidal wave. On 28 March 2005, the island of Nias was hit by the second most powerful earthquake in the world since 1965 and twelfth most powerful ever recorded. At least 800 people were killed and hundreds of buildings destroyed. An earthquake caused another tsunami on Java in July 2006.

◄ Mount Bromo is an active volcano that lies in the province of east Java. There was a minor eruption here in 2004. The last major eruption was in 1966.

THREE REGIONS

Geographically, Indonesia can be divided into three regions: the Sunda Shelf, the Sahul Shelf and the Lesser Sundas. The Sunda Shelf includes the islands of Java, Madura, Sumatra and Borneo, which are surrounded by shallow

▲ Many of the hillsides on the island of Bali are terraced and used as rice paddies. Terracing helps to reduce the amount of soil that is washed off the hillsides during heavy rainstorms.

seas. It extends from Malaysia to Thailand, Vietnam and Cambodia. About twenty thousand years ago, a land bridge joined these islands to the mainland of Asia, so they have plants and animals in common.

The province of Papua lies in New Guinea and, together with the nearby Aru islands, forms part of the Sahul Shelf. This stretches south to the Australian coast. The Lesser Sundas are a group of islands that separate the Sunda and Sahul shelves. They include Maluku and Sulawesi and the islands of Nusa Tenggara. Here the surrounding seas are up to 5,000 m (16,404 ft) deep, which indicates that these islands were never joined to another land mass.

Focus on: Krakatoa

In 1883, a volcanic eruption on the island of Krakatoa was so violent that it blew the island apart. The eruption was five times more forceful than the explosion caused by the atomic bomb that was dropped on the city of Hiroshima, Japan in 1945, and it could be heard thousands of kilometres away. It created a tsunami that destroyed more than 160 villages along the coasts of Java and Sumatra and killed about 36,000 people. Ash and lava poured out of the volcano in such huge quantities that these deposits formed new islands.

RIVERS AND LAKES

Most Indonesian people live near water, either on the coast or by rivers and lakes. The largest rivers, including the Mahakam, Martapura and Barito, are found in Kalimantan and they provide important routes to and from the mountainous interior. There are about 30 major rivers in Papua, most of which rise in the Maoke and Jayawijaya mountains; they include the 400-km (249-mile)-long Baliem River.

The largest lake in Indonesia is Lake Toba in Sumatra. It covers 1,145 sq km (442 sq miles) and is surrounded by steep mountain cliffs. Lake Tempe in Sulawesi is also large but is shrinking fast because of the build-up of silt from soil erosion in the surrounding area. Some parts of the lake are less than 2 m (6.5 ft) deep and they dry up completely during the dry season.

▲ The warm, clear seas that surround many of the Indonesian islands, as here near Sulawesi, provide perfect conditions for coral reefs. The reefs support a rich fish population, which is an important source of food for local people.

CLIMATE

Indonesia straddles the Equator, which means that it has a tropical climate. The coastal plains are hot and humid all year round, with an average temperature of 28°C (82°F). The climate is cooler inland, where temperatures average about 26°C (79°F), and cooler still in the higher mountain regions, where temperatures average about 23°C (73°F).

Indonesia has a monsoon climate: a wet season followed by a dry season. Most parts of the country experience their wet season between

November and March, when the winds blow from the north-west. It begins to rain at about midday each day and continues for a few hours. The dry season lasts from about June to October, when the winds blow from the south and east. Some areas, such as Maluku, have their wet season from March till August.

The lowland rainfall ranges between 1,700 mm and 3,200 mm (70 in and 126 in) per year, while mountain rainfall can reach 6,100 mm (240 in) a year. The highest rainfall occurs in the mountainous regions, such as west Sumatra, the interior of Kalimantan, inland Java, and parts of Papua and Sulawesi. Here the average rainfall call be 6,000 mm (236 in) or more. By contrast, the driest parts of the country, for

▼ This young girl uses a large banana leaf to shelter from the heavy tropical rain in Lombok. Brief but heavy rainstorms occur most days in the coastal regions.

example, the coastal plains of the Lesser Sunda islands and parts of Java, have an annual rainfall of less than 1,000 mm (39 in). Some years the rainfall can be exceedingly low and crops can fail.

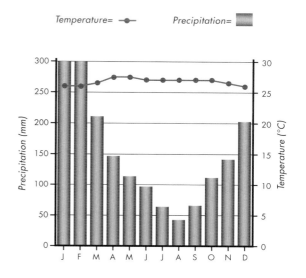

▲ Average monthly climate conditions in Jakarta

CHAPTER 4

Population and Settlements

Indonesia is the world's fourth most populous country. In 2006 the population stood at over 245 million and it is increasing at a rate of 1.5 per cent per year. About 29 per cent of the population are aged 14 years or under, which means that the population figure will continue to increase for some time to come. By contrast, in the UK the rate of increase in 2005 was just 0.24 per cent, with less than 18 per cent of the population aged 14 or under.

Although Indonesia's population is growing quickly, the rate of increase has slowed down slightly from a high of 1.8 per cent per year during the 1980s. A number of factors have caused this small reduction in growth, including improvements in education and the government's successful family planning programme.

MIGRATION TO THE CITIES

Indonesia's population is unevenly distributed – some areas are heavily populated while others have a small population. For example, 60 per cent of the population (about 145 million people) live on Java, Bali and Madura, but these islands represent just 7 per cent of the land area. Papua has 22 per cent of the land area but barely 1 per cent of the population.

Since the 1970s there has been a migration of people from rural areas to the cities in search of work. There is therefore a large urban population. By 2003, 46 per cent of Indonesia's population lived in urban areas, compared with 22 per cent in 1980. During the late 1990s, the urban population was growing at an estimated 3.6 per cent per year, more than twice as fast as the population in rural areas. This rapid growth

► Most houses are built on stilts, such as these on Sumbawa Island. This prevents the houses from flooding during heavy rains and provides ventilation. The space underneath the house is a useful storage area.

means that most cities are overcrowded and the infrastructure is unable to cope. The migrants often end up living in the large squatter settlements that have sprung up around the cities, where there are makeshift houses and no services, such as water and electricity.

MAJOR SETTLEMENTS

Jakarta in western Java is Indonesia's capital city, with a population in excess of 13 million, and is the main centre for industry and commerce. Other major cities include Surabaya in east Java, which has a population of about

► There are many slum areas in Jakarta where people live crowded together in very poor conditions. Here the shacks have been built on stilts beside a dirty canal. Although the water is polluted with sewage it is probably used for washing, cleaning and cooking.

Population data

📂 Population: over 245 million

📂 Population 0-14 yrs: 29%

📂 Population 15-64 yrs: 66%

📂 Population 65+ yrs: 5%

📂 Population growth rate: 1.2%

📂 Population density: 116.1 per sq km/300.6 per sq mile

📂 Urban population: 46%

📂 Major cities: Jakarta 13,194,000
                 Bandung 4,020,000
                 Surabaya 2,735,000

Source: United Nations and World Bank

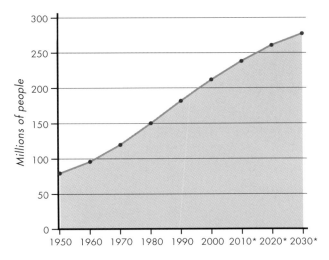

* Projected population

▲ Population growth, 1950-2030

▲ The Dayak people live in Borneo. Each village builds a few large community long-houses using local materials such as wood, bamboo and palm leaves. This Dayak woman is weaving a basket from palm leaves.

4 million and is an industrial centre and port. Semarang in central Java is a major port and commercial centre for the region. Bandung in west Java is an important centre for technology and aircraft manufacturing. Medan in northern Sumatra is a growing industrial centre based on agriculture and low-cost energy. Makassar is the capital city of south Sulawesi and is the main gateway to eastern Indonesia.

ETHNIC GROUPS

There are many ethnic groups living in Indonesia. The largest of these is the Javanese, who represent 45 per cent of the population and live mainly in central and eastern Java. The Sundanese live at the western end of Java and make up 14 per cent of the population. Other important groups include the Madurese, from Madura, who make up 7.5 per cent of the population and the ethnic Malay, who are spread through several areas and make up another 7.5 per cent of the population.

Among the ethnic groups on Sumatra are the Acehnese from the north, Bataks from around Lake Toba, and the Minangkabau from the western highlands. There are a number of ethnic groups on Sulawesi too, including the Minahasans, the Makassarese and the Bugis (known as seafarers) who live along the southern coasts. Kalimantan is populated by more than 200 groups, most of which are either tribes of the Dayak people, or ethnic Malay. There are also several million Indonesian Chinese. These people emigrated to Indonesia from China. Some have been settled in Indonesia for many generations, while others have only recently arrived.

ETHNIC TENSIONS

There has long been tension between Indonesians and those Indonesians of Chinese origin. The Chinese live mostly in the urban areas. Traditionally they have been successful in business and enjoy a higher standard of living than other Indonesians. This has led to resentment by other Indonesians. During 1997 and 1998, many Indonesians blamed the

Chinese for the country's economic problems and violent clashes occurred causing many thousands of Chinese to flee the country.

Violence has also flared up between Christians and Muslims in western Java, Ambon and parts of the Moluccas. Three years of fighting in the Moluccas resulted in about 5,000 deaths and caused 750,000 people to flee the islands. The fighting finally ended in 2002, when the two sides signed a peace deal. Ethnic violence has also occurred in Kalimantan, where the native Dayak people have resented the influx of migrants from Madura as part of the government's transmigration programme (see box below).

▼ Most food is bought and sold at traditional open air markets.

Focus on: Transmigration

From the 1950s, Indonesia's transmigration programme involved moving families from the overcrowded regions of Java to less densely populated islands. In the early 1970s, the programme gained the support of international donors, such as the World Bank. Since then, hundreds of thousands of families have been moved to Sumatra, Kalimantan, Sulawesi, Maluku and Papua. However, many of the indigenous people have resented the migrants and there have been violent clashes. In 2001, the Dayaks of Kalimantan killed thousands of Madurese migrants and the government was forced to evacuate many Madurese for their own safety. The government also let the migrants down by making promises of land, services, schools and transportation, many of which were not fulfilled. In 2000, the programme was halted because of rising costs and a shortage of suitable sites for resettlement; but the tension between the indigenous people and the migrants continues.

CHAPTER 5

Government and Politics

The government of Indonesia is faced with the challenge of balancing the needs of a very diverse country and maintaining unity. It also needs to tackle the problems of widespread corruption, human rights abuses and demands from several provinces for more self-rule and even independence. Other issues facing the government include poverty and terrorism.

GOVERNMENT ORGANIZATION

The government operates under a constitution that was first established in 1945. It is based on Pancasila, or the Five Principles; these include a belief in one god, a just and civilized society, the unity of Indonesia, democracy, and social justice for all Indonesians. There have been changes to the constitution over the years, most significantly in 2002 when the president was allowed to be elected directly by the people and the structure of the People's Consultative Assembly was altered to allow more regional representation.

The president is the chief of state, head of government and the supreme commander-in-chief of the armed forces. The national legislature is the People's Consultative Assembly. This has two chambers: the House of

▼ President Susilo Bambang Yudhoyono came to power in 2004. In May 2005 he met President George W. Bush for talks at the White House in Washington DC, USA.

Representatives (Dewan Perwakilan Rakyat, or DPR) and the Regional Representatives' Council (Dewan Perwakilan Daerah, or DPD). The DPR is the more powerful chamber as it approves all the laws and submits bills to the president for approval. The DPD was created in 2004 to represent the provinces, and its authority is limited to regional issues. Each of the 32 provinces has an equal number of democratically elected representatives. Each province has a governor, appointed by the president. The provinces are subdivided into districts (*kabupaten*) and sub-districts (*kecamatan*). As part of a move to decentralize the government, the districts have been given more responsibilities including health, education, agriculture, transport, industry and environment.

POLITICAL ORGANIZATIONS

While President Soeharto was in power there were three political organizations: Golkar (the ruling political organization), the Muslim-

▲ This woman is voting in the presidential elections in October 2004. It was the first time the Indonesian people had been able to vote in a direct presidential election.

backed Development Unity Party (Partai Persatuan Pembangunan, or PPP), and the Indonesian Democratic Party (Partai Demokrasi Indonesia or PDI). Since Soeharto's fall in 1998, more than 100 new political parties have been formed, including the Democratic Party led by Susilo Bambang Yudhoyono.

CORRUPTION

Corruption has been a problem in Indonesia ever since independence. An estimated US$2.35 billion are believed to have been 'lost' as a result of the misuse of state funds and bribery. Some groups claim that President Soeharto was the most corrupt political leader the world has seen for the past 20 years. However, the government elected in 2004 has taken action to stamp out corruption.

REGIONAL SELF-RULE

One of the constitution's Five Principles, national unity, is being challenged because several provinces want more self-rule. One such region is Papua, the easternmost province. Here the separatist group, the Free Papua Movement, has been fighting for independence since the 1960s. In 2002, the government of Megawati Sukarnoputri approved self-rule, giving the province control over its day-to-day affairs. The government also allowed Papua to retain much of the revenue from its natural resources and to change its name from Irian Jaya to Papua. However, the government has failed to establish self-rule. Instead, the province has been divided into two and there is a directly elected governor and a regional legislature. In 2005, the Indonesian government set up the Papuan People's Council to represent the views of the tribal peoples; but little progress has been made towards self-rule and the unrest continues.

The influx of large numbers of migrants and of people fleeing conflict in other parts of Indonesia has added to the problems in Papua. The indigenous Papuans are mostly rural and Christian, while most of the migrants are urban and Muslim, so there are many conflicting interests.

In the strongly conservative Muslim province of Aceh, an increase in self-rule has resulted in the adoption of Sharia (traditional Islamic) law. The Indonesian government is not an Islamic government that follows Sharia law, but many of its members are Muslims. However, in 2002 it allowed the provincial government of Aceh formally to adopt Sharia law, which had been used unofficially for many years. This strict Muslim code has specific rules on alcohol, dress and personal conduct.

▼ Although these Papuan tribal people live in the remote village of Jiwika in the highlands of Papua, they were still able to vote in the parliamentary elections in April 2004. Some Papuans travelled for many days to reach the polling stations.

HUMAN RIGHTS

The Indonesian government elected to power in 2004 campaigned on human rights issues. However, groups such as Human Rights Watch (an international non-governmental organization) have found evidence that there are still a number of obstacles to be overcome. For example, members of the armed forces continue to carry out arrests and beatings of civilians, detainees are tortured while they are in police and military custody, and protesters in Aceh and Papua are badly treated. The legal system is still corrupt, and this means members of the police and military are often not held to account for their actions.

▶ Female members of the Free Aceh Movement, photographed in 2001. These women have been trained to use weapons and they fight alongside the male separatists. Over the years, support for the separatist movement has grown and the Indonesian government has moved additional troops into the region to fight against the rebels.

Focus on: Tribal rights

The traditional way of life of many indigenous people is under threat from the influx of migrants and extensive deforestation (see page 55). Often the rights of indigenous people are ignored. In order to have a bigger voice in politics, the different indigenous peoples of Indonesia have formed an alliance. In 1999, they set up the Aliansi Masyarakat Adat Nusantara (AMAN) – Indigenous People's Alliance of the Archipelago. This alliance is supported by a number of international non-governmental organizations. Many indigenous groups were affected by the tsunami of December 2004, and AMAN has worked to make sure that the survivors are not resettled away from their tribal lands and that their way of life is preserved. AMAN is also campaigning for more self-rule for indigenous people; it is working to ensure that they have more control over the management of their natural resources.

CHAPTER 6

Energy and Resources

Indonesia is rich in natural resources. There are oil and natural gas fields as well as reserves of tin, bauxite, copper and precious metals. There are extensive forests and rich soils for agriculture.

OIL AND GAS

Most of Indonesia's oil and natural gas fields are found along the coast of Sumatra, in Kalimantan and in the seas around it. In 2005, Indonesia produced about 80 per cent of South-east Asia's oil. About 33 per cent of the world's liquefied gas comes from Indonesian gas fields. The government controls all oil and gas exploration and production through the state-owned oil company, Pertamina. Foreign companies, mostly from Europe and North America, can only operate in Indonesia through partnership agreements with Pertamina.

Oil production reached a peak of about 1.5 million barrels a day during the late 1990s.

Since then, production has fallen to 1.07 million barrels per day. This is because some of the older oil fields have dried up and there has been a lack of foreign investment. The domestic demand for oil has risen, so that Indonesia is now a net importer of oil. This costs the economy US$1.2 billion each year. Unless new

 Did you know?

The oil industry in Indonesia is one of the oldest in the world. Oil was discovered in northern Sumatra in 1883. Its discovery led to the formation of a new oil company, called the Royal Dutch Company for Exploration of Petroleum Sources in the Netherlands Indies. In 1907 this company merged with Shell Transport and Trading Company, a British company that was searching for oil in Kalimantan. The new company was called Royal Dutch Shell. Today, Royal Dutch Shell is one of the world's leading oil companies.

◀ During the 1970s, a large natural gas field was discovered off the coast of Aceh, near the town of Lhokseumawe. As a result, a huge oil terminal and petrochemical complex was built there.

oil fields are discovered, it is likely that Indonesian oil reserves will be depleted by 2020. However, gas production is high, and in 2002 Indonesia produced 70.4 billion cu m (2.5 trillion cu ft) of natural gas.

MINING

Mining contributes about 10 per cent to Indonesia's Gross Domestic Product (GDP). After Malaysia, Indonesia is the world's largest producer of tin. Most of the reserves are found on Bangka and Belitung islands in Sulawesi and in the Java Sea. Bauxite (the ore for aluminium) is produced on Bintan Island, while coal is mined on Sumatra, nickel on Sulawesi, and copper, silver and gold on Papua. Indonesia has increased its production of minerals by establishing joint ventures with US and UK companies. For example, British Petroleum (BP) and Rio Tinto carry out most of the coal mining.

► Workers extract sulphur from the slopes of an active volcano in east Java. They dig it out by hand and carry it down the slopes in baskets to a collection point. This is a hazardous job, and the workers wear no protection. Factories buy the lumps of yellow sulphur for use in manufacturing.

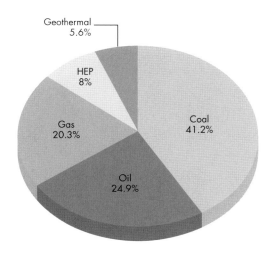

▲ Electricity production by type

Geothermal 5.6%
HEP 8%
Gas 20.3%
Coal 41.2%
Oil 24.9%

Energy data

🗁 Energy consumption as % of world total: 1.4%

🗁 Energy consumption by sector (% of total):

Industry:	18.5
Transportation:	18.7
Agriculture:	1.7
Services:	1.4
Residential:	58.8
Other:	0.9

🗁 CO_2 emissions as % of world total: 1.2

🗁 CO_2 emissions per capita in tonnes p.a.: 1.4

Source: World Resources Institute

ALTERNATIVE ENERGY SOURCES

The government is keen to develop alternative energy sources to reduce dependence on fossil fuels and help tackle the problem of air pollution (see page 54). Hydro-electric power (HEP) provides about 8 per cent of the country's electricity. One of the largest HEP dams is on the Asahan River in Sumatra. Given the country's mountainous landscape and high rainfall, there is much potential for the generation of HEP. Small-scale HEP projects are important because they provide power to remote mountain villages that lack an electricity supply. As a result of government grants, small wind turbines and photovoltaic panels (which convert light energy into electricity) have been supplied to some villages. Biogas is another important source of energy, especially in rural areas. It is a mix of gases produced by rotting organic wastes in an underground chamber, which can be used for cooking and heating.

AGRICULTURE

About one-fifth of Indonesia's land is either cultivated for crops or used for timber plantations. In 2005, agriculture accounted for 15 per cent of GDP. There are many small farms that provide much of the country's food. Rice is the staple food and in 2004 the yield was 53 million tonnes (52.16 million tons). Other important crops are cassava, coconuts, maize, peanuts, sweet potatoes, soybeans and sugarcane. A number of high-value crops are grown for export on large agricultural estates. Indonesia is the world's largest producer of cloves, the second-largest producer of rubber and the fourth-largest coffee grower. Other export crops include tea, cocoa, tobacco, sugar, and palm oil.

▼ In November 1999, the slopes near the village of Ubud are worked by hand as it is difficult to get machinery on to the terraces.

FISHING

Indonesia has a large fishery. The total catch in 2001 was 5.1 million tonnes (5.02 million tons), of which one quarter came from fresh water. The catch is made up of many types of fish, including tuna, carp, anchovy and scad as well as shrimp and prawn. About 90 per cent of the fishermen use traditional methods, such as nets, hooks and lines, and their fish is caught and sold locally. The remaining 10 per cent are commercial fishermen with large boats and they account for half the catch, most of which is exported. The production of farmed prawns for the European market has increased, and coastal mangrove swamps have been cleared to make space for the prawn ponds.

FORESTRY

Just under 60 per cent of the country is covered in hardwood forest, much of which is state owned. Indonesia is a major exporter of tropical hardwood and the largest exporter of plywood. Demand for wood has increased, especially from other Asian countries such as China and Japan. This, together with the deregulation in the trade in unfinished wood products such as plywood, has resulted in even more felling. Forestry is poorly controlled and illegal logging is a major problem (see page 59). The prevention of illegal logging is difficult to achieve, but the developed countries that buy these illegal products could do much to stop these exports by boycotting timber that does not come from legally logged forests. Consumers, too, could check the source of any timber they buy. Unfortunately, most of the forests are not managed in a sustainable way and the careful maintenance of this valuable resource is one of the country's most pressing issues. The Indonesian Ecolabelling Institute is setting up a timber certification scheme which will indicate if the timber comes from a sustainably managed forest.

▲ This woman is planting teak tree seedlings at Walanbenote community teak tree nursery on Muna Island, Sulawesi. It is important that felled trees are replaced to ensure a supply of timber for the future.

Focus on: Bird flu

There are millions of chickens and ducks in Indonesia, many of which are kept in the backyards of rural and urban homes. The deadly H5N1 strain of avian influenza ('bird flu') arrived in late 2003 and has since spread across two-thirds of the country killing millions of birds, including those kept for the poultry trade. Indonesia is preparing an early bird flu warning system to speed up the reporting of any outbreaks.

CHAPTER 7

Economy and Income

During the 1980s and 1990s Indonesia's economy grew, mostly as a result of the supply of cheap oil and gas. By the mid-1990s, Indonesia had become one of the best-performing Asian economies. It suffered a major setback, however, in 1997 because of the Asian Currency Crisis (see box opposite). Indonesia's economy only started to recover in 2000 and, by 2005, the annual growth rate had risen to 5 per cent, similar to that of Malaysia.

MANUFACTURING AND INDUSTRY

The industrial and manufacturing sector has grown over the last 40 years and in 2005 contributed 44 per cent to the GDP. Indonesia's main industries are petroleum, natural gas, mining, cement, chemical fertilizers, rubber and timber. Oil and gas were once major sources of export earnings but, in 2004, Indonesia became a net importer of oil. The country had been used to cheap supplies of fuel, but the imported oil was much more expensive. Initially the government subsidized the price of fuel to keep costs down, but as the global oil price increased in 2005 the predicted cost of the subsidies rose to a staggering US$11 billion. In October 2005, the government took action and increased the cost of fuel by 126 per cent. This caused inflation to rise to 17 per cent in 2006 and economic growth to fall.

SERVICE INDUSTRIES

Another major area of the economy is the service industry, which contributes 41 per cent to GDP. This sector is expanding fast and is made up of government services, transport, communications, finance, tourism and food. There are a large number of workers in this industry but many, such as the drivers of motorized taxis, street vendors and rubbish recyclers, are poorly paid. Most of these workers have little in the way of job security.

◀ Manufacturing is an important earner of foreign currency. These sports shoes are being made at a factory at Tangerang on Java in 2006. They are manufactured under licence and will be exported to Europe and North America.

▶ In 2005, the clean-up following the tsunami was a massive operation. These boys are collecting oil drums that have washed up on the coast near an oil refinery. The oil company pays them for every drum they find.

Economic data

🗁 Gross National Income (GNI) in US$: 248,007,000,000

🗁 World rank by GNI: 22

🗁 GNI per capita in US$: 1,140

🗁 World rank by GNI per capita: 137

🗁 Economic growth: 5.0%

Source: World Bank

GROWING WORKFORCE

Indonesia's main areas of employment are agriculture (40 per cent), services (38 per cent) and industry (17 per cent). Women make up about 40 per cent of the workforce. The rapidly expanding population means that the workforce is growing too. In 2003, the total workforce numbered 107 million, up from 60 million in 1980. Each year, several million new jobs are needed if the unemployment rates are not to increase.

Focus on: The Asian Currency Crisis

In 1997 there was international concern that many of the fast-growing Asian countries, such as Indonesia, had very large debts. This anxiety caused a fall in the value of the rupiah, the Indonesian currency, which in turn made it more difficult for the government and businesses to pay their foreign loans. Many businesses became bankrupt and millions of people lost their jobs. The International Monetary Fund (IMF) came to the rescue with a massive loan, but in exchange the government had to make efforts to cut spending and reform the financial sector. However, the crisis deepened in 1998 when the IMF claimed that President Soeharto was not carrying out the reforms, and the loan was stopped. Inflation soared and the situation became far worse. More than half the population was living in poverty and there were demonstrations in the cities. Eventually, in May 1998, Soeharto resigned. Since then, the economy has slowly recovered but levels of poverty still remain high.

Most of the manufacturing industries are based in Java, where the dense population provides the workforce and where there is a reasonable transport network. However, the government is attempting to direct investment and job creation away from Java by establishing free-trade and industrial zones elsewhere. The main zone is Batam Island, which lies across the Straits of Malacca from Singapore, an independent country at the tip of mainland Malaysia. Batam Island has fast developed into an international port and industrial centre. It is one of the country's wealthiest cities and is expanding rapidly (by more than 30 per cent in 2003). The international zone on Batam Island has already attracted substantial foreign investment, and similar zones are being considered for Kalimantan and Sulawesi.

MIGRANT WORKERS

The increase in the workforce and the lack of jobs has forced millions of Indonesians to look for work overseas. This is especially true in the case of women, who make up 75 per cent of all migrant workers. The money that migrant workers send back to their families represents important revenue for the economy. As many as 1.5 million Indonesians work in Malaysia, but there are thousands of others working in the Middle East, Hong Kong and Singapore. The men work in construction and agriculture while the women usually work as cleaners and cooks in private houses. The jobs are usually low paid and the hours are long. For example, there are about 200,000 Indonesian domestic workers in Malaysia and they typically work up to 18 hours a day, seven days a week, earning less than US$0.25 per hour. Many are forbidden to leave their workplace and some employers refuse to pay their workers until the end of their contract. There are a number of employment agencies in Indonesia that arrange the jobs, but they are poorly regulated and ignore the abuse that the workers suffer.

▼ A number of the major car manufacturers have assembly plants in Indonesia. This worker is welding parts to a car frame at the Japanese-owned Honda factory at Karawang in west Java. However, car sales have fallen in Indonesia and the workforce is being reduced.

In addition, there is a lot of illegal migration of workers who travel to other countries without the proper documents. Illegal workers suffer even more abuse than other migrant workers.

RISING POVERTY

About 10 per cent of the workforce are unemployed and an estimated 16.7 per cent live below the poverty line of less than US$17 a month. The government is trying to tackle poverty through poverty reduction committees that work within the community. These administer government grants to the poorest villages to enable them to develop and help individuals learn new skills and set up businesses. New finance schemes have been set up to offer farmers loans so they can develop their land.

Did you know?

The government intends to spend about US$1.5 billion in 2007 on improving conditions in about 70,000 villages and subdistricts. This will create around five million new jobs.

▲ As well as legal migrants, many illegal Indonesian migrants work in Malaysia. In October 2004 the Malaysian government ran an amnesty scheme which encouraged illegal migrants to return to Indonesia. They would then be able to obtain the necessary documents to become legal workers.

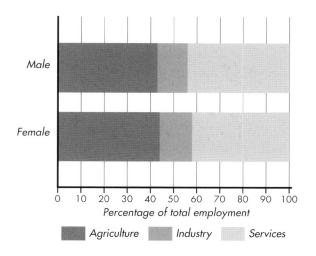

Percentage of total employment

■ Agriculture   ■ Industry   ■ Services

▲ Labour force by sector and gender

CHAPTER 8

Global Connections

Until 2004, Indonesia's relationships with some of its close neighbours were 'chilly', especially with Australia and Malaysia. The authoritarian government of Soeharto was suspicious of other countries and did not encourage close ties. Since the 2004 elections, Indonesia has been trying to improve its international standing. The president has participated in international summits such as the Association of South-east Asian Nations (ASEAN, see page 37) and Asia Pacific Economic Co-operation (APEC) summits and has held talks with neighbouring countries.

TERRITORIAL DISPUTES

Indonesia has far more coastline than most other countries (about 54,716 km/34,000 miles). In 1980 it claimed as territory all the waters surrounding its islands to a distance of 22 km (13.7 miles) from the coastline. In addition, it claimed an exclusive economic zone extending to 370 km (230 miles) in which it controlled fishing and geological rights. Not surprisingly, this move caused territorial disputes with its neighbours. Australia disputed the rights to the continental shelf off the coast of Timor, an issue that was finally resolved in 1991 with an agreement that allowed Australia and Indonesia joint access to the area. Disputes over boundaries between Indonesia and Singapore were settled in 2005.

In 2002, Indonesia and Malaysia took their territorial dispute of the Sipadan and Ligitan islands (off the coast of Kalimantan) to the International Court of Justice. The court decided in favour of Malaysia, but since then there have been further disputes over the rich

► In November 2005 the leaders of the Asia-Pacific Economic Co-operation summit met in Pusan, South Korea to discuss a range of issues, including their response to a possible epidemic of bird flu. In the foreground are Prime Minister Junichiro Koizumi of Japan (in grey robe) and President Susilo Bambang Yudhoyono of Indonesia (in yellow robe on right).

oil deposits in the seas around the islands. Warships from both countries moved into the area in 2005. Malaysia is managing the islands, but this is still disputed by Indonesia.

Indonesia's dispute with China over the Natuna islands in the South China Sea has still to be resolved. In 1993 China presented a map of its claims to territories in the South China Sea. The map included the Natuna islands together with much of the economic zone claimed by Indonesia. The gas reserves in this region are among the largest in the world, so both countries are claiming the territory.

COMBATING PIRACY

The Straits of Malacca between northern Sumatra, Malaysia and Singapore are one of the busiest shipping lanes in the world. They have been a subject of territorial dispute for years. Indonesia and Malaysia lay joint claim to the waters while other countries, notably the USA, consider them to be international waters. Most

▲ In the Straits of Malacca, naval patrols have been increased to stop the threat of piracy. These Indonesians were 'arrested' as part of a naval exercise involving Indonesia, Malaysia and Singapore in May 2000.

countries would prefer the straits to be classed as international waters because of their importance to world trade. However the threat of piracy is forcing Indonesia, Malaysia and Singapore to put aside their differences and work together. Piracy has been a problem in the straits for hundreds of years, but recently the number of attacks has increased. In 2000, there were a record 220 attacks. There are fears that terrorists could target the straits too, as it would be relatively easy to sink a ship in the shallowest part and block the shipping lane. As a result, Indonesia, Malaysia and Singapore have agreed to join forces and patrol the straits.

Indonesia has suffered from several terrorist attacks since 2002, including bomb explosions

◀ On 12 October 2002, bombs exploded in a nightclub area in the popular tourist resort of Kuta on the island of Bali. Over 200 people were killed and many more were injured. Here emergency workers remove victims from the scene.

in Bali in 2002 and 2005 and the bombings of the Marriott Hotel in Jakarta in 2003 and the Australian Embassy in 2004.

Countries such as the USA and Australia have urged the Indonesian government to address the threat of terrorism. The USA in particular has encouraged Indonesia to take an active role in regional security and has provided it with military assistance. However, this assistance is given on condition that Indonesia improves its record on human rights abuses. Since 2002, the Indonesian police force has arrested and successfully charged 40 terrorists, most of whom were Indonesian Islamic radicals linked to Al-Qaeda.

WORKING WITH AUSTRALIA

Indonesia's relationship with Australia, one of its close neighbours, has had its ups and downs. The government of Soeharto was deeply suspicious of Australia, as the Australians supported the people of Aceh and East Timor.

In 1999, Australia led the UN peacekeeping force in East Timor. The 2002 Bali bombing killed 88 Australians, more than any other single event in the country since the Second World War, and this led to close co-operation between the police forces of Australia and Indonesia. There were further improvements in 2005, when President Yudhoyono and Australian Prime Minister John Howard agreed to co-operate over fighting terrorism, drugs, illegal migration and people smuggling. But in 2006 relations reached an all

? Did you know?

Since the 2004 tsunami (see page 13), there have been international efforts to set up an early warning system to give countries time to evacuate their citizens from at-risk areas. Two early warning buoys have been deployed off the coast of Sumatra. They are connected to pressure sensors on the seabed which detect any movement caused by earthquakes.

time low when Australia granted asylum to a group of 42 refugees from Papua who claimed that the military was carrying out 'genocide' against the Papuan people. The Indonesian government claimed that this move was giving support to the separatist movement in Papua and demanded the refugees be returned. Australia responded by granting the Papuans a protection visa, which means that the Papuans can stay in Australia for three years.

ASEAN

A major part of Indonesia's foreign policy is its membership of the Association of South-east Asian Nations, an organization formed in 1967 by Indonesia, Thailand, Malaysia, Singapore and the Philippines to work on economic, social and cultural issues. Since then, Brunei, Vietnam, Laos, Burma and Cambodia have also become members.

▶ On 14 November 2003, Australian United Nations peacekeepers lower the UN flag during a farewell ceremony in Suai district, East Timor, after their tour of duty there.

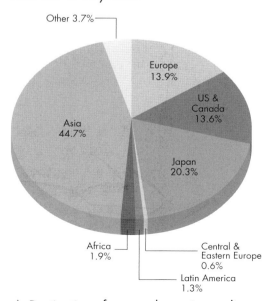

▲ Destination of exports by major trading region

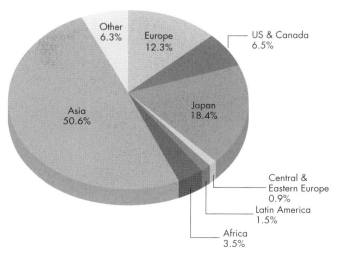

▲ Origin of imports by major trading region

CHAPTER 9

Transport and Communications

Travelling around Indonesia can be difficult because of the number of islands and their mountainous interiors. Nevertheless, good inter-island transportation is essential to the economy of the country.

ISLAND-TO-ISLAND TRAVEL

Air services fly between about 470 local airports, although some of these are little more than dirt landing strips. The national carrier is Garuda, which has international and domestic routes. Merpati Nusantara Airlines has mostly domestic routes and some international routes.

Ferries and other sea links are a common means of travelling between the islands. There are more than 300 registered ports for international and inter-island trade, including Batam, Cirebon, Jakarta, Kupang, Palembang, Semarang, Surabaya and Makassar. There are frequent ferry services between neighbouring islands, and across the Straits of Malacca to Malaysia and Singapore. In addition, there are more than 4,000 traditional sailing boats and about 1,000 motorized vessels that sail between the islands carrying goods and passengers.

There are nearly 22,000 km (13,670 miles) of inland rivers and other waterways. Boat services on these waterways provide essential transport to the inland regions. For example, the only way to reach the remote interior of Kalimantan is to use a long-boat (a shallow boat fitted with a high-powered engine).

◄ The 2004 tsunami destroyed the coast road that connected Banda Aceh and other towns with the rest of Sumatra, making travel difficult. In 2005 a new ferry service was set up from Banda Aceh to provide an alternative form of transport.

► Although travel on the commuter trains into Jakarta is relatively cheap, many people prefer to travel for free by sitting on the roof or clinging to the sides. Unfortunately a number of people fall to their deaths each year.

RAIL AND ROAD

Indonesian State Railways operate a limited train network serving Java and parts of Sumatra. The main route is between Jakarta and Surabaya but there are also rail links between Jakarta and Semarang, Yogyakarta and Solo. Commuter trains called *kereta api* run several times daily between Bogor and Jakarta. These basic trains are crowded and dirty, and many people sit on top of them to avoid paying fares.

Outside the main cities the road network is poor. Many of the roads in rural areas are little more than dirt tracks. There are long-distance bus services linking most of the major cities. It is possible to travel all the way from Banda Aceh in western Sumatra to Bali, although it takes several days and involves numerous buses and ferries.

Transport & communications data

- ▷ Total roads: 368,360 km/228,898 miles
- ▷ Total paved roads: 213,649 km/132,761 miles
- ▷ Total unpaved roads: 154,711 km/96,137 miles
- ▷ Total railways: 6,458 km/4,013 miles
- ▷ Major airports, paved runways: 161
- ▷ Cars per 1,000 people: 12
- ▷ Mobile phones per 1,000 people: 138
- ▷ Personal computers per 1,000 people: 14
- ▷ Internet users per 1,000 people: 67

Source: World Bank and CIA World Factbook

CITY TRANSPORT

Most of Indonesia's cities suffer from traffic congestion. The modes of transport are varied and include cars, taxis, buses, mopeds and numerous *bajaj* and *becaks*. *Bajaj* are motorized rickshaws that carry between two and five passengers.

There are more than 20,000 *bajaj* in Jakarta alone and each one is restricted to travelling in a specific part of the city. *Becaks* are people-powered rickshaws that were banned from Jakarta in 1994 because they tended to cause traffic problems. They are still found in other cities. There are also minibuses which carry ten or more passengers and they are a common way of travelling between the city centre and the suburbs.

COMMUNICATIONS

In the past it proved almost impossible to establish a good communications network across Indonesia, and many remote villages were cut off from the rest of the country. However, the arrival of new technologies such as satellite phones, mobile phones and the Internet is changing communications. Now it is possible for villagers in remote places such as Kalimantan to have satellite phones and Internet links. Mobile phone coverage is improving too, especially in the rural areas. These developments also enable people to keep in contact with family members working overseas.

MEDIA AND THE INTERNET

Until 1990, the television and radio networks were controlled by the government through the state-owned TV station, TVRI. Now there are more than 40 private TV stations, and they provide viewers with a greater choice of programmes. Soeharto's government maintained a tight control on newspapers and magazines and censored any content that was critical of either the president or the

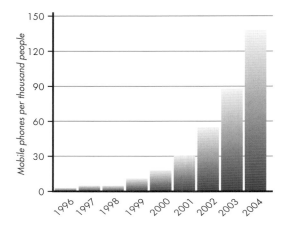

▲ Mobile phone use, 1996-2004

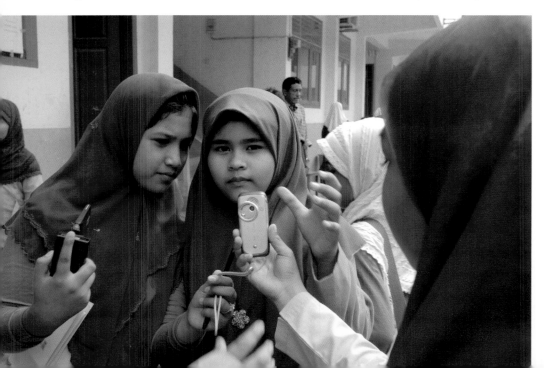

◀ As in Europe and North America, the mobile phone has become a 'must-have' item among young people, who are keen to own the latest model.

► About two-thirds of Indonesian people use an Internet cafés, such as this one in Block M shopping centre in Jakarta.

government. For example, in 1994 the government withdrew the licences of three of the country's leading magazines because of articles they had published. Since Soeharto left office in 1998, censorship has been relaxed and there are many more publications in existence.

Focus on: Jakarta's traffic problems

Jakarta has a massive traffic congestion problem, caused by the four million or so vehicles that crowd its streets. These vehicles are also responsible for much of the air pollution in the city. Since 1992, a 'three-in-one' rule has been in operation during the rush hour, which means that access to certain roads is restricted to cars with three or more passengers. Now the city has started an ambitious programme to build a rapid transit system comprising an underground network, new railway links, a monorail and bus routes. Construction on the bus routes started in 2003. But these massive engineering projects caused even more traffic congestion. Finally the new measures are beginning to work, and the bus routes are attracting thousands more passengers each year.

The first Internet services became available in 1995. Since then, access to the Internet has increased and there are numerous online services including those offering newspapers and shopping in the national language, Bahasa Indonesia. However, the level of access to the Internet in Indonesia is far behind that of Singapore and Malaysia. This is because few Indonesians own their own computer, and between 60 and 70 per cent of Internet access in Indonesia is provided by Internet cafés. There is debate in Indonesia, at government and local level, about whether it is necessary to restrict access to certain kinds of websites on the Internet, such as those showing pornography and those linked to terrorist groups.

 Did you know?

In 2005, President Yudhoyono told a small meeting of people that if they thought the government did not care about their problems they should call him on his mobile phone. He gave out his number, which was broadcast everywhere by the media. Within minutes the president's mobile phone was overwhelmed with a barrage of complaints!

CHAPTER 10

Education and Health

Indonesia's population is putting pressure on social services such as education and health. The government is faced with the challenge of providing education and healthcare to a young and rapidly expanding population, many of whom are living in poverty.

PRIMARY SCHOOLING

An important government goal following independence was to provide every child with at least six years of primary schooling, and this has been achieved. During the 1970s, some of the oil revenue was used to build new primary schools and fund education programmes. By the late 1980s, about 40,000 primary schools had either been built or had their existing buildings improved. This provided a new generation of schoolchildren with a firm foundation for their education and, during the 1990s, these children progressed through the educational system to university. As a result of these educational programmes, literacy is relatively high: 94 per cent of adult males and 86 per cent of adult females are now literate. However, the quality of education varies throughout Indonesia and there are problems with supplying adequate facilities, well-qualified teachers and textbooks in remote areas.

Since 1990, compulsory education includes six years of primary schooling and, by 2008, an additional three years at junior secondary school will also be compulsory for all students. An additional three years at secondary school are optional.

Around 87 per cent of children attend primary school at six years of age. It is not completely free, as parents have to pay for books and uniforms. Most schools have classes in the

◀ In 2005, children play outside their Islamic primary school on the outskirts of Banda Aceh.

► A teacher helps students with their classwork at a secondary school in Timor.

morning and all children are expected to do several hours of homework. Primary school children also attend a special class in school to study Pancasila, the guiding principles of Indonesian society (see page 22). They must pass exams in this class in order to progress to the next grade. Islamic schools, called *madrasas*, are growing in popularity as they offer free education. However, in *madrasas* the pupils are taught only about Islam and the Koran.

SECONDARY AND BEYOND

Slightly fewer than 60 per cent of primary school children continue to junior secondary school for three years. Then they go to secondary school for a further three years, assuming they pass the entrance exam. Afterwards they can go to university. However, university courses are very expensive and generally only the wealthier pupils can afford to go. Indonesia has more than 50 state-run universities and more than 1,000 private universities. The largest and most important universities are the University of Indonesia in

Jakarta, Gajah Mada University in Yogyakarta and Padjadjaran University in Bandung.

In the past, more boys attended school than girls, but in 2005 the percentage of boys and girls attending primary and junior secondary school was very similar. Slightly fewer girls than boys go on to higher education.

Education and health

- Life expectancy at birth, male: 65.5
- Life expectancy at birth, female: 69.3
- Infant mortality rate per 1,000: 31
- Under five mortality rate per 1,000: 41
- Physicians per 1,000 people: 0.1
- Health expenditure as % of GDP: 3%
- Education expenditure as % of GDP: 1%
- Primary net enrolment: 87%
- Pupil-teacher ratio, primary: 20
- Adult literacy as % age 15+: 90

Source: United Nations Agencies and World Bank

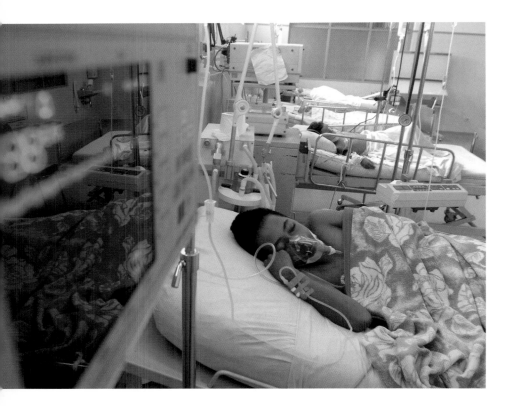

◀ These patients in a hospital in Jakarta are being treated for dengue fever. In 2004 there was an outbreak of dengue fever, a disease carried by the mosquito. Several hundred people died and many thousands were infected before the outbreak was brought under control.

HEALTH

In recent years the Indonesian government has focused on providing basic healthcare to the population to reduce the high death rate among young children. Improvements have been achieved by the setting up of public health centres called *puskesmas*. These are supervised by doctors who provide maternal and child care, vaccinations and disease control. Mobile *puskesmas* have been important in bringing free healthcare to many remote villages.

The poorest people get free healthcare. Wealthier people use the growing number of private clinics, while some travel to Singapore and Malaysia where the private services are of a higher standard.

CHANGING LIFESTYLE

Over the last 20 years or so, the lifestyle of Indonesians has changed, with fast foods appearing in the diet. There are now many more fast food outlets and smoking has become popular. One in four people smokes, and sedentary lifestyles are common in urban areas where many people have office-based jobs and where there are few open spaces for taking

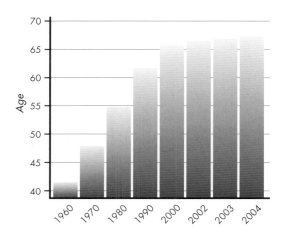

▲ Life expectancy at birth, 1960-2004

exercise. All these changes are adversely affecting the health of millions of Indonesians and the incidence of smoking-related respiratory and coronary illnesses is rising. Traffic accidents also cause many deaths and injuries.

IMPROVING CHILD HEALTH

Although the infant mortality rate has fallen to 31 deaths for every 1,000 live births in 2005, it is still double that of Malaysia. Diarrhoea is a major killer and in recent years cases of diarrhoea have doubled among women and young children. This illness has been linked to poor sanitation and lack of basic healthcare.

The level of poverty is rising and is causing more cases of malnutrition, especially among young children. One of the key signs is anaemia, a low level of iron in the blood caused by a poor diet. More than 60 per cent of children in Java are anaemic, while in some of the remote villages there have been cases of marasmus. This is a disease that is more commonly seen in malnourished children in Africa, and is characterized by a 'pot-belly'.

► The use of herbal remedies, called *jamu*, is common in Indonesia. The remedies come from roots, flowers, bark, nuts, herbs and spices.

Focus on: Tuberculosis

More than half a million new cases of tuberculosis (TB) are reported in Indonesia each year and 175,000 people die from it every year. Indonesia ranks third out of the 22 countries of the world with a high level of the disease. TB accounts for 7 per cent of all disease in the country, compared with just 4 per cent in neighbouring countries.

A bacterial lung disease, TB can be treated with antibiotics, although the process is lengthy and expensive. The incidence of TB is often linked to HIV. In 2003, HIV infections leapt more than 60 per cent to 210,000 new cases. Experts believe this rise is a result of the practice of re-using syringes in rural clinics to save money.

CHAPTER 11

Culture and Religion

Indonesia has a rich culture of art and music based on many civilizations and religions. During the 1950s and 1960s, the arts in Indonesia were influenced by politics. A popular form of art was social realism, in which paintings reflected social issues. Djoko Pekik is well known for his paintings depicting the day-to-day problems of poor people in Indonesia. In 1966 many socialist artists were killed during the backlash against communists; some went into exile while others, including Pramoedya Ananta Toer (see box opposite), were arrested. In place of social realist art, traditional art was encouraged and artists with a modernist approach were discouraged. In 1998, the resignation of Soeharto meant that artistic freedom was restored and artists were free to explore all forms of art.

DANCE AND MUSIC

Dancing has an important role in Indonesian culture, especially on the islands of Java and Bali, where dance and drama are combined. Traditional dance dramas are based on epic Hindu poems. The female dancers wear elaborate headdresses, colourful costumes and grow long nails to emphasize their hand movements. The dancing is usually accompanied by *gamelan* music, which is played on flutes, zithers and percussion instruments, such as gongs, xylophones and drums.

Today, there are many influences from the West in art and dance. Modern choreographers blend Western with traditional Indonesian dance to reach a younger audience. For example, the *sendratari* is a traditional dance drama in which the performers use modern costumes and movements. Indonesia is famous for its textiles and batik, but today Indonesian artists are experimenting with Western techniques too, for example by combining oil paints and batik.

◀ In Denpasar, Bali in 2005, dancers with elaborate headdresses are taking part in the Melasti ceremony, in which the victory of good over evil is celebrated.

paints and batik.

The most popular music is *dangdut*, which can be heard on the streets and in shops and bars. It is described as a modern dance rhythm influenced by rock, Indian film music and urban Arab pop. One of the most famous *dangdut* singers is Rhoma Irama, who sings about Islam, social issues and family values.

▲ Puppets such as these have been used in shadow theatres in Java for more than 1,000 years. The puppeteer manipulates the puppets so that their shadows move across a white screen.

Focus on: Pramoedya Ananta Toer

One of Indonesia's greatest authors is Pramoedya Ananta Toer, who was born in 1925 while Indonesia was under Dutch rule. He was arrested and imprisoned three times because of his writing: between 1947 and 1949 by the Dutch over his anti-colonial views, then for nine months in about 1955 by the Sukarno government for publishing a book that was considered too sympathetic to the ethnic Chinese. In 1966, Toer was sent to the prison island of Buru for 14 years. While there, Toer told a story each night to his fellow prisoners to help them forget their suffering and hunger. After his release he published these stories in a set of four books called *Minke's Story*, about a young Javanese boy living in Dutch colonial times. The first book, *This Earth of Mankind*, was published in 1981 and immediately became a bestseller. The Soeharto government banned Toer's books, but pirate copies were widely read. He was shortlisted for the Nobel Prize for Literature in the year 2000. He died in April 2006.

LANGUAGE

Bahasa Indonesia is the official language of Indonesia. It is a version of Malay that was commonly used throughout Indonesia by traders. It is a very simple language with no verb tenses, noun genders or articles. It is important as it is a language that unifies Indonesia. However, Bahasa is spoken mostly by people in urban areas; in the rural areas, people tend to speak the language associated with their ethnic group. There are 580 other languages in use. Javanese, which originated on the island of Java, is spoken by about 45 per cent of the population, while 14 per cent speak Sundanese. Some languages are spoken only in a single village, for example Ruta and Soahuku from Seram Island. There is concern that some of these languages are spoken by so few people that one day they will be forgotten.

FOOD

The staple food of most Indonesians is rice, but on some of the eastern islands, maize, sago and root vegetables, such as cassava, taro and sweet potatoes, are the staples. Coconut is found everywhere and is processed for cooking oil; its milk and flesh are also used in many dishes.

Each province has its own style of cooking. Spices and hot chilli peppers are used widely, especially in west Sumatra and north Sulawesi. Javanese recipes use vegetables, soybeans, beef and chicken, while Sumatran dishes use more beef. Further to the east, fish is more prominent, either grilled or curried. Pork is a speciality in Bali, Papua and the highlands of north Sumatra and north Sulawesi.

 Did you know?

There are Padang restaurants everywhere in Indonesia, serving hot, spicy food dishes from Padang, west Sumatra. The waiter brings dozens of small plates with various dishes to the table and the diners can eat whatever they like. At the end of the meal, they are charged just for the food that they have eaten.

◀ A traditional Indonesian meal consists of rice together with a number of small meat or fish dishes.

► Independence Day is celebrated on 17 August. This is one of several festival days celebrated in Indonesia. Others include Idul Fitri at the end of Ramadan, which is celebrated by Muslims.

RELIGION

The majority of the people, 87.2 per cent, are Muslim, making Indonesia the country with the largest population of Muslims in the world. Indonesia's constitution guarantees freedom of religion and people are therefore allowed to follow the religion of their choice. More than 9 per cent are Christians, most of whom are Protestant. Hinduism was once common in Indonesia, but now most Hindus are found on Bali and in eastern Java. The Chinese minority follow a range of different religions. Some are Buddhists, but there are also Christian and Muslim Chinese. Some Chinese are Confucians, but until recently this was not a recognized faith. Some isolated communities in Indonesia are animist. Animists believe that animate and inanimate objects have a 'roh' or life-force and they practise ancestor and spirit worship.

Despite the freedom to follow different religions, there has been conflict between the different groups. For example, since 1999 clashes between Christians and Muslims on the Maluku Islands have claimed 6,000 lives. More fighting between religious groups has occurred in Poso in central Sulawesi.

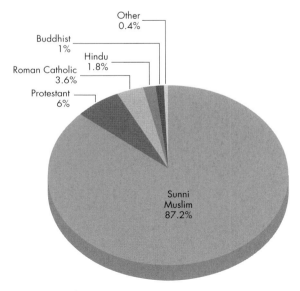

Other 0.4%
Buddhist 1%
Hindu 1.8%
Roman Catholic 3.6%
Protestant 6%
Sunni Muslim 87.2%

▲ Major religions

CHAPTER 12

Leisure and Tourism

Indonesians participate in a wide range of sports and leisure activities, both traditional and modern.

SPORT FOR ALL

The government is keen for people to participate in sports. National Sports Day is held each year on 9 September and is considered to be important for unity, as participants from all over the country take part. The government has sponsored a youth organization called *Karang Taruna*. A network of local leaders organize activities, such as sports and community work, for members of the *Karang Taruna*.

Among the most popular sports are badminton and tennis. Indonesian badminton players have dominated the sport internationally since the 1950s. When badminton became an Olympic sport at the 1992 Barcelona Olympics, Indonesia won all four gold medals. The country is successful internationally in other sports, too.

For example, the tennis team has won many regional trophies, while the women's archery team won the country's first Olympic medal at the 1988 Olympics in Seoul, South Korea.

FOOTBALL

Young people play football but there are few facilities, so they have to play on beaches or in parks with makeshift goals. In Papuan villages there is a communal ball that hangs in the goal net. Everyone is allowed to play a game of football as long as he or she replaces the ball in the net afterwards. There is a national football league. Since long-distance journeys are difficult and expensive, a team travels to a region where it plays a series of games before returning home.

TRADITIONAL SPORTS

Traditional sports in Indonesia include boat racing, kite flying, *pencak silat* (a form of martial arts similar to karate) and *sepak takraw*, or kick

► Most villages have a badminton court. All that is needed is a hard surface and a net. This court is in Bena village on the island of Flores.

volleyball. A cross between football and volleyball, *sepak takraw* is played on a badminton court. There are two teams, each made up of three players and a substitute. The aim is to keep a rattan ball in the air for as long as possible using any part of the body, except the hands.

LEISURE TIME

Indonesians love watching films at the cinema and there are cinemas in all but the smallest villages. Foreign films with Bahasa Indonesia subtitles are shown in the larger cities such as Jakarta, Surabaya and Denpasar. Many of Indonesia's larger cities lack recreational areas. In Jakarta, for example, land prices are high and in the past governments have not put much land aside for recreation. One of the few open spaces is found around the national monument located near the city centre. Each morning, thousands of people use this open space for taking exercise in the form of walking, jogging, cycling, aerobics and *t'ai chi* (a form of martial arts designed to improve balance and health).

▲ These people have just taken part in a mass parade of football dribbling through the centre of Jakarta to celebrate the final of the World Cup in 2002.

 Did you know?

Congklak is a popular family board game played on a wooden board with a series of small depressions along its sides. There are 98 markers, usually shells or pebbles, which are placed on the depressions. The two players move the markers in a game of strategy and skill to reach the 'home' depression.

TOURISM

Indonesia's long coastlines, palm-fringed beaches and coral reefs make it a major tropical holiday destination. Most of the tourists come from Singapore, Japan, Taiwan, Malaysia, Australia, Germany and the USA. Annual revenue from tourists is worth about US$5,226 million.

The holiday industry has experienced setbacks in recent years as a result of the 2002 Bali bombing and the SARS epidemic in early 2003. Tourist numbers recovered slightly in 2004, when almost 5.5 million international tourists visited Indonesia. But numbers fell again following the tsunami in December 2004 and the Bali bombings of 2005. The Ministry of Culture and Tourism has tried to encourage tourists by inviting international tour operators

▼ The seas around Indonesia are home to about 15 per cent of the world's coral reefs and the number of divers is increasing each year. The established centres are on Java, Bali, Nusa Tenggara and Sulawesi, but newer dive areas include the islands of Maluku, western Sumatra and Papua.

to visit. Indonesian embassies around the world have also been acting as unofficial tourism representatives by providing information about the country.

Tourism in Indonesia

- Tourist arrivals, millions: 5.321
- Earnings from tourism in US$: 5,226,000,000
- Tourism as % foreign earnings: 5.8
- Tourist departures, millions: 2.076
- Expenditure on tourism in US$: 4,570,000,000

Source: World Bank

BOROBODUR AND PRAMBANAN TEMPLES

Yogyakarta is one of Indonesia's main cultural centres because it lies close to the huge Borobodur (Buddhist) and Prambanan (Hindu) temples, which are both World Heritage sites. Borobodur was built between AD 778 and 850. Within a hundred years the temple was buried

beneath a mountain of volcanic ash from Mount Merapi. There it remained until 1814, when it was rediscovered by Sir Thomas Stamford Raffles. The temple was cleared of ash but it was damaged, so in 1975 a major restoration project was started with help from UNESCO. The temple was finally opened to the public in 1983. The Prambanan temple complex dates from the tenth century and contains temples dedicated to the Hindu gods Shiva, Vishnu and Brahma.

BEACHES AND VOLCANOES

Bali has long been a popular destination and is considered to be the 'jewel in the crown' of the Indonesian tourist industry. It has beautiful beaches, temples and picturesque rice terraces. However, the recent bombings have caused some tourists to stay away, and now the islands lying to the east of Bali, known as Nusa Tenggara, are attracting more visitors, especially the island of Lombok. These islands are well known as a top surfing destination. Another attraction is the large reptile, the Komodo dragon, which is found only on the island of Komodo. Some of Java's biggest natural attractions are its volcanoes, especially Mount Bromo. A popular tourist activity is a climb to the summit of Mount Bromo to see the sunrise.

ECOTOURISM

The Indonesian government is trying to encourage ecotourism, especially in the rainforest and coral reef areas. Ecotourism holidays allow people to get close to nature,

for example, by watching orang-utans in the rainforest or helping with turtle conservation projects in Sulawesi. Ecotourism puts money back into the local community and helps to provide employment in some of the more remote areas.

▼ The Komodo dragon is found only on the island of Komodo. This huge reptile can be very dangerous so the tourists are staying a safe distance behind it.

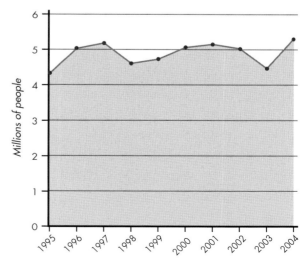

▲ Changes in international tourism, 1995-2004

CHAPTER 13

Environment and Conservation

Since independence, various Indonesian governments have focused on economic growth and paid little attention to the environment. Over the years there has been widespread environmental damage, in particular air and water pollution in Java and deforestation across Indonesia.

AIR POLLUTION

The large numbers of poorly maintained vehicles and the use of cheap, bad quality fuels mean that the air quality in most cities is very poor. The high level of small particles from exhaust in the air causes breathing difficulties, particularly among the elderly and those suffering from heart conditions. Jakarta is the third most polluted city in the world after Mexico City and Bangkok. Air quality is not improving; for example, in 2005 Jakarta experienced only 20 days of fresh air, compared with 21 days in 2003 and 25 days in 2002. In 2005, new laws were passed to control vehicle emissions and to require all public vehicles to run on LPG (liquefied petroleum gas) in an attempt to improve air quality.

THE THREAT FROM LEAD

The World Bank has identified exposure to lead as the greatest environmental threat to the health of Indonesians, especially children. Lead is found in the emissions of vehicles running on leaded fuels and from lead smelters, and in lead paints. Children are very sensitive to lead and it can adversely affect their mental development and behaviour. The Indonesian government started to phase out leaded fuels in 2001.

There is an increasing problem of hazardous waste from industry. There are few controls over its disposal, and much of it ends up in dumps in urban areas. Hazardous waste, for example computers containing toxic metals for recycling, is also exported by other countries, such as the USA, Japan and Singapore.

◀ Traffic jams during the morning rush hour are common in Jakarta. Many of the vehicles are poorly maintained and they pump out toxic exhaust gases.

► New roads are cleared through the rainforests of Kalimantan in order to bring in heavy machinery and take out the logs. The new roads open up more areas of forest for exploitation.

Companies in these countries find it cheaper to send their waste to Indonesia than to dispose of it at home. Some of the waste has been placed in landfill sites where the hazardous materials contaminate groundwater. These effects may be felt for many decades.

DEFORESTATION

In 1988 Dr Norman Myers, a leading ecologist, described the Indonesian rainforests as a biodiversity hotspot because of the vast numbers of plants and animals that live there. But these valuable forests are being cleared at a frightening rate. Between 1990 and 2005, more than one quarter of the country's forests were cleared.

The reasons for forest clearance are several. Trees are felled for their valuable hardwood, for veneers and for plywood to export. They are cleared for mining, and for new oil palm and rubber plantations; they are also cleared to provide land for migrant families and to supply wood pulp for the huge pulp and paper industry. Unlike many other countries of the world, in Indonesia the pulp and paper industry has not replanted forests but simply cleared

more primary forest. Another major cause of clearance is illegal logging (see page 59).

The continuing loss of forest and the abuse of the rights and customs of the indigenous peoples who live there has caused outrage around the world and there has been considerable international pressure on Indonesia's government to take action. In 2005, the government started to develop a strategy to manage the forests sustainably and to stamp out illegal logging.

 Did you know?

In 1997 huge forest fires caused by deforestation and drought spread across Kalimantan and Sumatra. The smoke from these fires increased air pollution levels across South-east Asia, and the pollution reached as far as Australia and Thailand. On 23 September 1997, the air pollution index hit a record 839 µg/m3 (micrograms per metre cubed) in Sarawak, Malaysia. The air pollution index is a measure of the mass of tiny particles of solid matter in the air from fires and vehicle exhausts. Usually, levels are well below 100. Levels of more than 300 are considered to be hazardous to health.

CONSERVATION

Of the 2,467 or so known species of amphibians, birds, mammals and reptiles found in Indonesia, about 30 per cent are endemic, that is, they are found in no other country. They are unique to Indonesia. This rich biodiversity makes it vitally important for Indonesia's habitats to be protected through various conservation programmes.

The first national park, Ujung Kulon National Park in Java, was established by the Dutch in 1921 to protect the endangered Javan rhinoceros. Today there are 50 rhinos, and their population remains stable. Patrols in the park and along the coast help prevent poachers from reaching the rhinos. Other endangered species in the park include the Javan gibbon (a small ape) and the banteng, a species of wild cattle.

Another protected area is Bukit Barisan Selatan on Sumatra, a remnant of rainforest surrounded by villages and farmland. In this

shrinking reserve there are 300 species of bird as well as Sumatran rhinos, tigers, elephants, sun bears, bearded pigs, tapirs, gibbons, rare orchids and rafflesia plants.

Other protected areas include Lorentz National Park in Papua, covering about 2.5 million hectares (6.2 million acres), Komodo National Park, that protects the Komodo dragons, and the Leuser Ecosystem in Aceh. The Leuser Ecosystem is a huge forested area and believed to be the last remaining place where elephants, rhinos, tigers, clouded leopards, and orang-utans can all be found living together.

Environmental and conservation data

- 📁 Forested area as % total land area: 59.7
- 📁 Protected area as % total land area: 12.5
- 📁 Number of protected areas: 965

SPECIES DIVERSITY

Category	Known species	Threatened species
Mammals	515	147
Breeding birds	929	114
Reptiles	745	28
Amphibians	278	n/a
Fish	4,080	68
Plants	29,375	384

Source: World Resources Institute

◀ In Jakarta, in 2006, this young boy is hunting for bits of plastic floating among the rest of the rubbish in the polluted river. He will be able to sell the plastic to earn some money.

▶ At dawn the sun rises over the volcanic landscape at the Bromo-Tengger-Semeru national park on the island of Java.

THREATS TO THE REEFS

Indonesia's coral reefs are among the most biologically rich reefs in the world, with about 1,600 species of fish and 480 species of coral. However, about half of them are facing a medium-to-high risk of damage. Healthy reefs are important. Not only do they support the fisheries but they also act as breakwaters to protect the coast from storm surges. The reefs are threatened by over-fishing and industrial wastes, sewage, fertilizers and pesticides. Silt makes the water cloudy, blocking the sunlight that corals need in order to grow. The soil erosion that follows deforestation increases the amount of silt carried by the rivers.

In 1998, the World Bank provided US$7 million for the Coral Reef Rehabilitation and Management Programme to promote environmentally sustainable development. Pilot projects were set up in Taka Bone Rate National Park in south Sulawesi and Lease Islands in Maluku. The programme has succeeded best when the communities have been allowed to manage their local reefs and where 'no-take' zones have been established to create sanctuaries for fish.

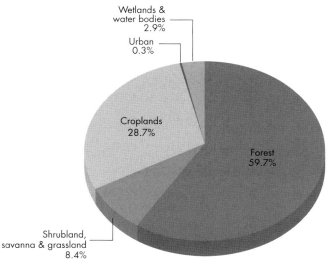

Wetlands &
water bodies
2.9%

Urban
0.3%

Croplands
28.7%

Forest
59.7%

Shrubland,
savanna & grassland
8.4%

▲ Habitat type as a percentage of total area

Focus on: The Green Coast Project

After the tsunami of 2004, conservation organizations led by Wetlands International, IUCN and WWF set up the Green Coast Project. The aim of the project is to restore coastal ecosystems such as mangrove swamps in the tsunami-hit Asian countries. This will provide the coastal communities of Sumatra with new fisheries and natural protection from storms, cyclones and future tsunamis.

CHAPTER 14

Future Challenges

Following his election in 2004, President Yudhoyono said he was committed to encouraging economic growth, creating jobs and beating poverty. Other issues facing Indonesia include combating illegal logging, fighting corruption, preventing terrorism and rebuilding those parts of Aceh and Nias damaged by the 2004 tsunami and 2005 earthquake.

▼ Fishing is an important industry in Aceh and aid programmes are financing the building of new boats and nets following the 2004 tsunami.

ECONOMIC PROBLEMS

In 2004, fuel subsidies (see page 30) cost the country as much as US$8 billion and meant that less money was available to fund social services and development projects. The abolition of the subsidies in autumn 2005 meant that the government could start investing in services such as healthcare, education, water and sanitation. But the government was soon faced with economic problems. The rise in fuel prices caused inflation, and since 2005 many businesses have gone bankrupt and people have lost their jobs. It is likely that growth will be slower in the short term, while businesses and the public adjust to the higher fuel costs. In the long term, the government must allow for lower production from its own oil and gas fields and increase the amount of electricity that is generated using renewable energy sources.

Various events have influenced the Indonesian economy. Although the tsunami in Aceh and the earthquake in Nias did not have a huge effect on the national economy (less than 0.5 per cent of GDP), the impact in these areas was severe. In Aceh, the damage was estimated at US$4.5 billion, although many of the costs of rebuilding will by covered by international donors. It will take many years for the economies of these regions to recover.

Terrorist incidents in 2005 reduced the number of tourists once again, especially in Bali where the tourist industry had only just recovered from the 2002 bombing. Then, in late 2005, Indonesia reported 16 cases of human avian influenza (bird flu) which sparked widespread panic. Once again, tourists stayed away.

► Mangrove swamps help to protect coasts from tidal surges. These workers in Aceh are potting up mangrove saplings which will be used to restore damaged mangrove swamps along the coast.

ILLEGAL LOGGING

There is no doubt that illegal logging is one of the most pressing issues facing Indonesia. Despite the tough government statements and new policies to fight illegal logging, the practice continues at an even faster rate. Regional self-rule is at the root of the problem, because each province manages its own forests and issues logging concessions. Existing laws are ineffective in stopping the activities of corrupt officials, many of whom work with powerful figures in organized crime. Some experts have warned that, if current rates of logging continue, there will be no forest left outside the national parks in fewer than 15 to 20 years.

Indonesia has huge natural resources in the form of hardwood forests, rich agricultural soils, reserves of oil and gas and valuable metals, such as copper, gold and tin. If the government can achieve its aims of eradicating corruption, reducing poverty and creating jobs and succeed in pulling the many different peoples together, Indonesia has the potential to become one of the richest countries in the world.

 Did you know?

The Indonesian government selected seven priority areas for 2006. They were:
1. Reducing poverty
2. Creating jobs and increasing investment and exports
3. Revitalizing agriculture and rural areas
4. Improving accessibility and quality of education and healthcare
5. Improving law enforcement, eradicating corruption and reforming bureaucracy
6. Improving security and defences
7. Reconstructing Aceh and Nias

Timeline

c.850 The Buddhist temple of Borobodur on the island of Java is completed.

1292 Explorer Marco Polo lands in Sumatra.

1511 Portuguese traders reach Indonesia.

1596 Dutch traders claim West Timor.

1623 The Dutch East India Company takes control of Indonesia.

1799 The Dutch East India Company closes down. Control of Indonesia passes to the Dutch government.

1815 Mount Tambora on Sumbawa Island erupts killing about 50,000 people and sending a cloud of volcanic dust around the world.

1883 The volcano Krakatoa erupts creating a 40 m (130 ft) tsunami in Indonesia's Sunda Strait, killing 36,000 people in Java and Sumatra.

1918 The Dutch set up the Volksraad in Jakarta.

1927 The Indonesian Nationalist Party is formed.

1942 Japan invades the Dutch East Indies and the Dutch colonial government surrenders to Japan.

1945 The Japanese army surrenders and Sukarno and Hatta declare independence for Indonesia. Indonesian nationalists spend the next four years fighting Dutch troops. East Timor remains under Portuguese control.

1949 Indonesia gains independence and Sukarno becomes president.

1965 Six army officers are assassinated causing rioting in the streets. There are mass arrests of communists and as many as 500,000 Chinese Indonesians are killed. Sukarno asks Soeharto to bring the country to order.

1967 Soeharto becomes president.

1969 West Papua becomes a province of Indonesia and is renamed Irian Jaya (becomes Papua in 2002).

1975 Portugal grants independence to East Timor, but Indonesian troops annex it. In the following months 600,000 are killed.

1994 Mount Merapi, an active volcano in central Java erupts violently, killing 43 people.

1997 The Asian Currency Crisis devalues the currency and results in demonstrations on the streets.

1998 Soeharto resigns and B.J. Habibie becomes president.

1999 Abdurrahman Wahid is voted in as the new president. East Timor votes for independence in a United Nations sponsored referendum. Anti-independence militia kill thousands of people and UN peacekeeping troops move in to East Timor.

2001 Ethnic violence in Kalimantan, where indigenous Dayaks force out Madurese migrants. Megawati Sukarnoputri is elected president.

2002 East Timor becomes independent.

12 October 2002 A car bomb explodes outside a nightclub in Bali, killing 200 and injuring 300, the worst terrorist act in Indonesia's history.

5 August 2003 A car bomb explodes outside the Marriott Hotel, Jakarta, killing ten people and wounding 149, including two Americans.

2004 Susilo Bambang Yudhoyono becomes president in the first-ever direct presidential elections.

26 December 2004 A powerful undersea earthquake off the coast of Sumatra creates a huge tsunami that floods coasts and kills about 130,000 people in Indonesia.

2005 A major earthquake hits the west coast of northern Sumatra. More than 1,300 people die, most of them on the island of Nias.

15 August 2005 Indonesian government and Aceh rebels sign a peace treaty in Helsinki to end nearly 30 years of fighting during which 15,000 people have been killed.

1 October 2005 Three bombs in Bali kill 23 people, including the bombers.

2006 Two earthquakes occur on the island of Java. The first hits the city of Yogyakarta in May, causing more than 6,000 deaths. The second earthquake in July occurs off the coast of Java. It is followed by a 3-m (9.8-ft)-high tsunami which kills around 700 people.

December 2006 The former spokesperson of the Free Aceh Movement, Irwandi Yusuf, wins the first direct election for governor of Aceh province.

Glossary

Archipelago A group of islands.

Authoritarianism A style of government in which the leader is not appointed in free elections and the people are subjected to strict controls and restricted freedom.

Bribery Offering or giving something of value (usually money) to influence the action of an official.

Colonial Relating to people settling in a different country from their own and applying their laws and language to that country.

Confucian A follower of the teachings of Confucius, a Chinese philosopher who lived from 551-479 BC.

Decentralize To distribute responsibility from central to regional government.

Democratic Party A political party founded in 2001.

Detention Being confined, usually for a short period of time.

Ethnic group People of the same cultural, racial or religious origins.

Genocide The deliberate destruction of an entire people or ethnic group.

Gross Domestic Product (GDP) The total value of goods and services produced within the borders of a country.

Indigenous Coming from a particular area.

International Court of Justice A court set up to settle disputes between members of the United Nations.

International Monetary Fund (IMF) An organization that oversees monetary co-operation between nations and lends money to countries that are experiencing financial difficulties.

International Union for the Conservation of Nature and Natural Resources (IUCN) A worldwide conservation network.

Literate Able to read and write.

Mangrove A tropical tree that grows in forests in swampy areas along coasts of tropical oceans.

Marasmus An extreme form of malnutrition caused by lack of protein and energy foods in the diet.

Militia A military group raised from the general population to assist the army in an emergency; or a rebel group acting in opposition to the regular army.

Net importer A country that imports more of something than it exports.

Organized crime A type of crime carried out by groups of people organized for the purpose, for monetary gain or political influence.

Plywood A sheet of wood made up of three or more thin sheets of wood bonded together with glue.

Realism A style of art in which the subject matter is shown as accurately and realistically as possible.

Referendum A vote among a group of people on a single issue.

Rickshaw A small, two-wheeled cart pulled by one person.

SARS Severe Acute Respiratory Syndrome, a respiratory disease that first appeared in China in 2003.

Separatists People that want to break away from the main group, for example, to form a separate country.

Sharia law Traditional Islamic law, based on the Koran and the teachings of the Prophet Muhammad.

Socialist A person who favours socialism, a political system based in theory on public ownership and the equal distribution of wealth.

Sustainable Capable of being maintained or repeated.

United Nations (UN) An international organization formed in 1945 to promote peace, security and economic development.

Western allies The countries that fought against Germany and Japan in the Second World War; they included the UK, the USA, Canada and Australia.

World Bank The sister organization to the IMF, the role of the World Bank is to lend money to countries when no other funds are available.

WWF A global, independent conservation organization, working in more than 90 countries.

Further Information

BOOKS TO READ

Countries of the World: Indonesia
Tristan Burton
(Evans Brothers, 2005)

Culture in: Indonesia
Melanie Guile
(Heinemann Library Australia, 2002)

Krakatoa: The Day the World Exploded:
August 27, 1883
Simon Winchester
(Penguin, 2004)

Nations of the World: Indonesia
Edward Horton
(Raintree, 2005)

Next Stop: Indonesia
Fred Martin
(Heinemann Library, 1999)

Among the Orangutans: Birute Galdikas Story
Evelyn Gallardo
(Chronicle Books, 1995)

USEFUL WEBSITES

www.indonesia.go.id/en/
The official website of the Indonesian
government, with many up-to-date
news stories.

www.noaanews.noaa.gov/stories2004/s2357.htm
Web pages about the Asian tsunami, with
animation showing its spread across the Pacific.

www.unicef.org/infobycountry/
index_28354.html
UNICEF website with a report on the situation
in Banda Aceh following the tsunami.

www.wwf.or.id/index/php?language+e
Website describing the work of the WWF in
Indonesia.

http://www.geology.sdsu.edu/how_volcanoes_
work/Krakatau.html
http://news.bbc.co.uk/1/hi/sci/tech/4972522.stm
Web pages providing detailed information
about the eruption of Krakatoa.

Index

Page numbers in **bold** indicate pictures.

About the Author

Sally Morgan is an experienced author of children's books and has written on a wide range of topics including nature, science, geography and environmental issues. She is particularly interested in wildlife and conservation and has travelled to South-east Asia on many occasions to photograph rainforest wildlife.